CHRISTOPHER COLUMBUS

❖ **Why They Became Famous** ❖

CHRISTOPHER COLUMBUS

Lino Monchieri

Translated by Mary Lee Grisanti

Silver Burdett Company

Acknowledgments
English translation adapted for Silver Burdett Company by Vincent Buranelli.

We would like to thank Professor J.K. Sowards, Department of History, Wichita State University; David A. Williams, Professor Emeritus, Department of History, California State University, Long Beach; and Craighton Hippenhammer, Cuyahoga County Public Library, Ohio for their guidance and helpful suggestions.

Library of Congress Cataloging in Publication Data

Monchieri, Lino.
    Christopher Columbus.

    (Why they became famous)
    Translation of: Colombo.
    Summary: An account of Columbus's four transatlantic
voyages.
        1. Columbus, Christopher — Juvenile literature.
    2. Explorers — America — Biography — Juvenile literature.
    3. Explorers — Spain — Biography — Juvenile literature.
    4. America — Discovery and exploration — Spanish —
Juvenile literature. [1. Columbus, Christopher.
    2. Explorers. 3. America — Discovery and exploration —
Spanish] I. Title. II. Series.
    E111.M7613   1985   970.01'5   [92]   84-51622

    ISBN 0-382-06851-3 (Library Binding)
    ISBN 0-382-06981-1 (Softcover)

© Fabbri Editori S.p.A., Milan 1982
Translated into English by Mary Lee Grisanti for Silver Burdett Company
from Perche Sono Diventati Famosi: Colombo
First published in Italy in 1982 by Fabbri Editori S.p.A., Milan

CONTENTS

The Grand Admiral

When the drummers and trumpeters sounded their instruments, the immense crowd quieted down as if a huge, invisible hand had silenced them.

It was an April day of the year 1493, and the people of Barcelona filled the streets to witness an event unique in the history of Spain — unique in the history of the world.

At the heart of the tree-shaded square, a solemn procession approached. Men and women of the court, dressed in the splendid costumes that the state occasion required, marched slowly beneath the banners of Aragon and Castile, two Spanish regions united under the rule of King Ferdinand and Queen Isabella. With the officials and dignitaries of the court walked Christopher Columbus, the admiral of the Great Ocean, governor of the islands, and viceroy of the king.

The crowds stared at a number of men behind Columbus. These men were copper-colored, clad in costumes adorned with feathers and gold, and carrying cages in which parrots fluttered and squawked. Europe was getting its first glimpse of the American Indian. Columbus had brought the Indians back with him from his great voyage of discovery. He called them "Indians" because he thought he had reached the East Indies near China and Japan. The name stuck even after it became clear that Columbus had discovered a new world far from the East Indies.

The people were in a festive mood. As Columbus passed, the spontaneous joy of the nation was clear in the cries of: "Long live the admiral!"

Columbus and his men had landed at Palos on the Spanish coast some weeks earlier. From there he had sent a letter to the king and queen in Barcelona, describing his voyage and asking to be received at court. Ferdinand and Isabella were pleased to agree. The news spread rapidly. And so the people of the city were ready for their joyful celebration when he arrived.

The procession made its way through the streets of Barcelona to the royal palace. Here, King Ferdinand and Queen Isabella were sitting on their thrones. Usually, they remained seated while they greeted their subjects. This time, however, they rose to their feet to greet Columbus, which showed their respect for him. Like everyone else, they were thrilled by his achievement.

He knelt to kiss their hands, after which they insisted that he rise and sit beside them. Then they questioned him about his voyage across the Atlantic, about the lands he had seen, and about the human beings he had met. They were impressed by the Indians he presented to them. The Indians were proof that he had been to strange places.

When the meeting ended, the king, the queen, Columbus and the rest went to the royal chapel for a religious ceremony of thanksgiving for the safe return of the sailors from their momentous voyage. After that, Columbus was cheered again in the streets as he made his way to his lodgings.

The reception in Barcelona made up for all the problems the Great Navigator had faced from the time he first proposed to reach the East by sailing west. They had been very difficult problems. He had been disappointed over and over again. He had even thought of leaving Spain and asking the king of France to support his expedition. But now, all that was over. Everyone knew he was right when he sailed boldly out into the Atlantic. He enjoyed the fame that had come to him.

"From the City of Genoa"

Christopher Columbus used to say: "I am from the city of Genoa." It was a boast often made by those who were born in "Genoa the proud." Their city dominated the northwest coast of Italy, and was a thriving commercial center facing the Mediterranean Sea. Ships carried cargoes from Genoa to French and Spanish seaports. They crossed the Mediterranean to North Africa to buy and sell in cities like Tunis and Tripoli. Foreign vessels were constantly arriving at the wharves of Genoa. Thus, as a boy, Columbus was familiar with ships and sailors.

He was born in Genoa in 1451. The exact date of his birth is unknown. His father was a weaver, and his mother was the daughter of a weaver. The whole family worked at turning sheep's wool into cloth. They must have been close to one another as a family because Christopher later brought his brothers, Bartholomew and Giacomo, to the New World to assist him.

Christopher Columbus grew up to be tall, broad-shouldered, red-haired, and freckled. He was very religious. He had not gone to school, and virtually everything he knew of books he had to find out for himself.

He went to sea in his teens as a hand aboard vessels carrying wool and cloth along the Italian and French seacoasts. His first long voyage was to Tunis. By then he had decided to leave the family clothing business and become a sailor. He felt the heady call of the open sea. "I love the taste of salt spray in my face," he told a friend, "and the feel of a deck rising and falling under my feet, and the sight of tall ships rocking at anchor in the seaports of the Mediterranean."

Columbus sailed to the Greek island of Chios aboard a Genoese merchant ship on at least one occasion. In 1476 he got his first glimpse of the Atlantic Ocean, the broad, turbulent body of water extending west from Europe into the unknown where European sailors had never been. He was with a trading fleet that sailed out of the Mediterranean through the Pillars of Hercules (the Strait of Gibraltar), and into the Atlantic. The commander of the fleet intended to land part of his cargo in Portugal, and the rest in England and Flanders (modern Belgium).

One of Europe's many wars was raging. A French flotilla attacked the fleet and sank a number of ships. One of them was the ship on which Columbus served. Thrown into the water, he seized a floating oar and managed to swim six miles to the coast of Portugal through huge waves, despite the fact that he had been wounded in the battle.

At that time Portugal was the leading maritime nation. It had the best ships, and sailors came from all over Europe to sail in them. Columbus decided to stay in Portugal and see if he could make his fortune. In 1477 he sailed with a Portuguese trading fleet to Iceland, stopping at Galway on the west coast of Ireland.

This voyage raises an interesting question. It has been said that in Iceland Columbus heard how Leif Ericson, in the year 1000, reached a place across the Atlantic that he called "Vinland," which we now know to have been on the coast of North America. The story is probably false because Columbus never mentioned the Ericson voyage when he insisted that his plan to cross the Atlantic was practical. He never said: "The Vikings have crossed the Atlantic. So, I can do it, too." He obviously knew nothing about Leif Ericson and Vinland.

In 1478 Columbus married Filipa Perestrello in Lisbon. A son, Diego, was born to them a year or two later. They lived for some years in the Madeira Islands off the North African coast where her brother was the governor. The rest of the time they were in Lisbon.

Columbus continued to go to sea. In 1483 he was the captain of a ship trading with the Gold Coast of West Africa. That was a period when Portuguese sea captains were pushing down the African Coast to see how far south the continent extended. Some geographers thought Africa ran all the way down to the South Pole. But in 1488 Bartholomew Dias reached East Africa after rounding the Cape of Good Hope. In 1498 Vasco da Gama followed the same route, crossed the Arabian Sea, and made landfall on the coast of India.

Meanwhile, Columbus had sailed in a different direction in 1492, not south along Africa but west across the Atlantic.

The idea of making a spectacular voyage may have come to him when he was a boy in Genoa. We may imagine him listening to the tales of seafaring men returning from voyages across the Mediterranean to North Africa and up the north Atlantic to England or even Scandinavia.

We may imagine one sailor saying: "Why don't you ship out with us? You'll work hard, but you'll see the world and learn to be a sailor. Being at sea is the best life for a boy your age. That's how I started!"

Then Columbus may have pressed this sailor with questions about such problems as steering by a compass, unfurling the sails, and what to do when a storm made the ship pitch and toss.

Whether or not such a conversation ever took place, we know that Columbus went to sea in his youth. As we have seen, he rose to be a captain and explored the African coast in the service of Portugal.

When did Columbus first think of abandoning African waters for a transatlantic voyage? Perhaps it was while he, Filipa, and Diego were living in the Madeira Islands.

First of all, he knew that Portuguese expeditions had discovered the Madeiras, the Azores, and the Canaries — all islands far out in the Atlantic. Why not push farther out into the ocean in search of new discoveries?

Secondly, strange objects, pushed by the Gulf Stream, floated ashore on the island beaches from time-to-time. There was driftwood made up of tree trunks, branches, bushes, and uprooted plants of types never seen before. Europeans could not know as we do, that this driftwood came from the Caribbean. On one occasion two dead bodies came in with the tide. Their features were not European. It was thought that they might be Chinese — an idea that could have convinced Columbus that China was not far away across the Atlantic. Of course the bodies were really those of American Indians.

Columbus was not the only one to ask the meaning of these strange objects floating in from out in the Atlantic. He was not the only one to think of looking for their place of origin. The trouble was that no other sea captain dared to challenge the terrors of the Atlantic.

"The distance is too great and the ocean is too rough," one Portuguese captain reported. "Whoever sails too far into the Atlantic will never return!"

Everyone agreed with this conclusion. Everyone except Christopher Columbus.

He held to his great idea of crossing the Atlantic. His problem was to convince others that the voyage he had in mind was practical. He had to make them believe that he could do it. After that, he had to find financial backing for his expedition.

Before we see how Columbus gained support for his voyage, we must reject one myth. According to the myth, everyone believed the earth was flat until Columbus said the earth was round. Washington Irving wrote this in his *Life of Columbus,* and his scene of the Great Navigator contradicting the flat-earth men spread the myth wherever his biography was read. Washington Irving was a great American writer, but on this point he had the facts wrong.

The fact is that long before Columbus, all geographers, astronomers, and other learned people knew the earth was shaped like a sphere. Aristotle the philosopher and Ptolemy the geographer said so in ancient times. Two centuries before Columbus, Dante, the Italian poet who wrote the *Divine Comedy,* described the earth as round. Later writers all agreed on this.

But there was a more immediate proof. The Portuguese sea captains pushing south along the African Coast knew they were traveling on a curve.

Familiar stars in the night sky vanished suddenly behind them. New stars appeared suddenly over the bows of the ships. This could happen only because the curve of the earth blotted out the old stars and allowed the new stars to be seen. If you look at a globe, you will see clearly how and why this happened.

Again, when a ship approached another on the high seas, the first thing to come in sight was the top of the mast. Then the sails would gradually appear, followed by the hull of the ship. If the earth were flat, the whole ship would come into view at the same time.

All those who discussed exploring expeditions knew the world was round. Therefore, nobody ever warned Columbus: "If you sail westward across the Atlantic, you will fall off the edge of the earth."

Why, then, did Columbus run into so much opposition? It was not because of the *shape* of the earth. It was because of the *size* of the earth. The opposition thought the earth was much larger than Columbus did.

The question was whether the sailing ships of the time were strong enough for a transatlantic voyage. Could they carry enough provisions for the crew? Columbus thought the answers were "yes" because the ocean was not very wide.

He gathered books on geography and noted down their estimations of the distance from Europe to the Orient. He selected the smallest figures in order to show that the voyage would be a short one. Thus, he decided that the distance from the Canary Islands to China was 3,550 miles. That was well within the sailing capabilities of the ships he would command. The actual distance is 11,766 miles.

His opponents had a better idea of the true distance. That was why one of his critics declared: "Columbus, you have greatly underestimated the size of the earth. You can never sail all the way to the Far East."

Columbus was completely wrong. Yet, he never knew it. He thought he was in the East Indies when he was really in the West Indies. Except for the existence of the New World, he would have had to turn back. Or else, he would have been lost at sea.

Even though Columbus was a man with a vision, reality turned out to be better than his vision. True, he failed to reach the East Indies as he had intended, but he did something better. He discovered a new world.

The expedition Columbus dreamed of would require a number of ships, enough sailors to man them, food, and clothing. In short, the expedition would be quite expensive. Unable to pay the costs himself, Columbus would have to find someone to finance his expedition.

"Christopher, where are you going to find the money for your voyage?" asked his brother Bartholomew, who had come from Genoa to Lisbon.

"There is only one person who can approve the voyage and pay for it," came the reply. "I will go to the king of Portugal."

"That is the right thing to do," Bartholomew agreed. "King John has backed many exploring voyages. He may back yours."

King John II agreed to receive Columbus at the royal palace in Lisbon. The king sat at a table that held geography books and maps of the world. His experts on navigation were there to advise him.

Columbus explained his plan to sail from Portugal across the Atlantic to the East Indies. "You see, Your Majesty," he concluded, "the distance is not great. I can sail it."

The king looked around at his advisers. They shook their heads doubtfully. "The distance is much greater than Columbus thinks," said one.

"The voyage is impossible," said another.

"Well, I will appoint a special commission to look into the matter," the king replied.

The commission rejected the proposal. Then John II sent ships to sail out into the Atlantic and test Columbus's plan. The captains lost their nerve and returned to say that a voyage to the East Indies was impossible.

Columbus had traveled to Spain to seek help. But the failure of this trip to find financing for his expedition caused the king of Portugal to summon him back. Columbus returned to Lisbon with high hopes.

And then, in 1488, Bartholomew Dias rounded the Cape of Good Hope. The Dias voyage showed that India, the East Indies and all of the Orient could be reached by a route around the southern tip of Africa.

The king of Portugal now had no further need of Columbus. Why should the king support a voyage across the Atlantic, even if it could reach the East Indies, when his ships could reach the East Indies by sailing around Africa?

Columbus was informed that the king's answer was "no."

"Christopher, what will you do now?" Bartholomew asked.

"I will try somewhere else. There are other European kings who are interested in exploration — the kings of England and France, for example. However, I will go back to Spain first. Perhaps this time King Ferdinand and Queen Isabella will be in a position to accept my plan."

"Ferdinand and Isabella are enlightened monarchs," Bartholomew nodded. "Yes, you may well get a better reception at the Spanish court than you did at the Portuguese court."

"I will soon find out," was the answer.

Columbus returned to Spain in 1489. He already had friends there from his first visit in 1485. Indeed, he had met King Ferdinand and Queen Isabella. He had presented his case for a transatlantic voyage. His idea was still under discussion by experts at the Spanish court.

In 1485, after his wife had died, Columbus traveled for some time with his son, Diego, who was a small child. They took ships from Lisbon to Palos, a bustling Spanish seaport. Upon arriving there they walked to a Franciscan monastery located outside of the city. It was a long, dusty walk.

"Are you tired, Diego?" Columbus asked as they tramped along.

"Yes I am, father," the child admitted.

"And hungry and thirsty, no doubt?"

Diego nodded.

"Well, cheer up. We haven't far to go. I can see the walls of the monastery. I'm sure we can count on the hospitality of the Franciscans."

At the monastery, Columbus rang the bell. He and Diego waited until the porter arrived and asked who they were.

"I am Christopher Columbus, of Genoa. I ask your hospitality for my son and myself."

"We never turn travelers away," the porter said. "Come in and we will share what we have with you."

The head of the monastery greeted the two wayfarers. "We have only simple fare," he told them, "but you are welcome to it."

Columbus and Diego sat at a rough wooden table. They ate bread, cheese, and vegetables from the monastery garden. Columbus explained that he had come to Spain to see the king and queen.

"That may be difficult, Master Columbus," the monk said. "We Spaniards are engaged in a war with the Moors, who have occupied our land for centuries. Our victory will come as soon as we have retaken our land from the invaders. But the king and queen are unable to think of much else besides the fighting."

"It may take me some time to be granted a royal interview," Columbus agreed. "While I am waiting, I would like to leave Diego here at the monastery in your care. Would that be possible?"

"Of course. Diego can stay with us as long as you wish."

"Thank you. I feel relieved that my son will be in good hands while I am away at the court."

Columbus and Diego finished their meal. Then Columbus talked to the Franciscans about their simple life. He found that they were all very happy to be in the monastery. They enjoyed their work in the fields. They felt peace of mind at their prayers. They felt no desire to take part in the busy city life of nearby Palos.

Columbus was impressed because he, too, was very religious. He always kept in mind that he was named for Saint Christopher, the patron saint of travelers. He wore a Saint Christopher's medal wherever he went. He considered the medal a good omen of a safe journey.

"Why are you, a man from Genoa, here in Spain?" one of the Franciscans inquired.

Columbus shrugged. "I have been laughed at so often that I am almost afraid to tell you. The truth is that I hope to receive royal backing for a voyage."

The Franciscan stroked his beard. "A voyage? That should not be too difficult to arrange. Many Spaniards have sailed to Africa."

Columbus smiled. "The trouble is that I am not bound for Africa. I want to sail across the Atlantic to the East Indies."

The Franciscan looked startled. "No sea captain has ever done that," he pointed out.

"That is the problem," Columbus admitted. "I want to be the first. I want to show that it can be done."

"You sound very confident."

"I am confident. My difficulty is finding a royal patron who will share my confidence."

Columbus spent the night at the monastery. He departed the following morning, leaving Diego with the monks.

When he arrived at the palace Columbus was unable to see the king and queen at once. During the wait, he met a woman named Beatriz Enriquez de Harana. Since his wife was dead, there was nothing to prevent his marrying Beatriz if he wanted to. Whether or not he did is not known, but the two had a son, Ferdinand, who later wrote about his father's voyages to the New World.

At last, in 1486 Columbus received word that the king and queen would receive him in the city of Cordova. King Ferdinand was not interested in the planned voyage. Queen Isabella was the one who questioned Columbus about it. After hearing his passionate plea for royal backing, the queen asked her experts to consider the plan and report back to her.

"As you know, there is a war on," Isabella said to Columbus. "So, even if my advisers agree with you, I cannot approve so great an enterprise until the last Moorish stronghold in Spain has fallen to the royal armies."

"I trust it will be soon, Your Majesty."

The queen smiled. "So do we all, but the Moors are not easily defeated. They were a strong military power when they invaded Spain centuries ago. After crossing from North Africa by way of the Strait of Gibraltar, they occupied most of Spain. It has been a long, hard struggle to push them back."

"The royal armies now stand on the brink of success, do they not, Your Majesty?"

The queen nodded. "When we take Granada, that will end the war. But I cannot say when that will be. Still, I will keep you in mind."

"Your Majesty, I am grateful for your consideration," Columbus declared.

He left the royal conference quite hopeful. However, he felt that he had to accept when King John II of Portugal summoned him back to Lisbon.

"A bird in the hand is worth two in the bush," he thought, comparing the possibility of support in Spain with the greater hope in Portugal.

We have already seen how he waited in Lisbon, and how his hopes were dashed once and for all by the successful voyage of Bartholomew Dias around the Cape of Good Hope in 1488.

The Great Enterprise

Disillusioned in Portugal, Columbus journeyed back to Spain in 1489. After visiting the monastery near Palos to see Diego, he again sought a meeting with Queen Isabella.

The queen received him in a gracious manner. But the war against the Moors was still going on, distracting the attention of the queen as well as the king of Spain. And the queen's advisers still disagreed with Columbus. They insisted, rightly, that the earth was much larger than he thought.

"Pray be patient, Master Columbus," the queen urged him. "I cannot make a decision yet. My royal commission has not made its report."

Columbus bowed. "Your Majesty gives me hope," he said. "I will be patient."

While waiting for Isabella's decision, he went back to his books and maps. He spent many a long day checking his figures. Often he read far into the night by the light of flickering candles. Often he fell asleep at his desk as dawn was breaking.

More than ever he became convinced that his figures were correct. He could not believe that he was wrong about the size of the earth. In reality, his calculations made the circumference of the globe too short by one-quarter. No wonder he believed he could make a short voyage to the East Indies!

As he discussed his plan with geographers and merchants who had cargo ships on the high seas, he found a few individuals who favored an attempt to explore the Atlantic Ocean beyond the Canary Islands.

"Columbus, I do not know whether you are right or wrong," said one geographer. "But the Canaries, the Madeiras, and the Cape Verde Islands were unknown before ships sailed far enough out in the Atlantic to find them. Why should you not seek more unknown islands beyond them?"

Columbus had an immediate response. "Because I do not intend to look for unknown islands. I intend to find a new route to the East Indies!"

This was always his attitude with those he spoke to. He clung to his vision, and he would not accept anything less than full support for an expedition across the Atlantic.

That support would depend, at least in part, on the war against the Moors in Spain. Therefore, Columbus watched anxiously as the armed forces of Ferdinand and Isabella pushed southward, capturing one Moorish city after another.

"The war is going better than ever," a Spanish friend remarked. "When Granada falls, the way to the Mediterranean will be open. The last Moorish city will be ours. All of Spain will be liberated from the enemy."

"God grant a speedy victory to King Ferdinand and Queen Isabella," said Columbus.

"You sound like a patriotic Spaniard, Columbus."

"I wish Spain well, my friend, because I've been here so long. Also, as a Catholic I am happy to see Catholics defeat the infidels. I have a personal reason as well."

"I know. It's that voyage you're always talking about."

"It certainly is," Columbus declared emphatically. "The queen cannot approve my petition until the war is over."

"Even victory will not make her approval certain," the friend observed.

"No, the report of the queen's commission will sway Her Majesty," Columbus confessed. "I only hope the report is favorable to me."

In 1490 Columbus received another summons to appear before the king and queen. He hastened to obey. After greeting him, King Ferdinand allowed Queen Isabella to explain why they wanted to see him.

"The royal commission has submitted its report on the voyage you wish to make," the queen announced. "I am sorry to tell you that their report is unfavorable."

Columbus could not help showing his disappointment. "Then Your Majesty has decided not to support my expedition?"

"The king and I have not made our minds," Isabella replied. "The commission's report is not the last word. We may decide to give you our support in spite of it. But the whole affair is too complicated for us to decide now. We must get on with the liberation of Spain from the Moors."

"Will Your Majesty be good enough to tell me why the members of the commission ruled against me?" Columbus asked.

"They believe the voyage would take three years."

"They are wrong!" Columbus exclaimed. "I am quite sure I can reach the East Indies, explore the area, and return in one year!"

"It would be an excellent accomplishment for you if you could do it Christopher."

"And for Spain, too, Your Majesty!" Columbus anxiously pointed out.

"I agree, and that is why I am willing to listen to you again, but at another time."

The audience was at an end. Columbus withdrew. He went back to his lodgings wondering how long he would have to wait this time.

"Onward to the East from the West!"

Months passed. Columbus heard nothing more from the king and queen of Spain. The war looked as if it might drag on indefinitely. He therefore decided in 1491 to leave Spain and try his luck in France.

He went to the monastery to pick up Diego, whom he intended to take with him. While talking to the head of the Franciscans, Father Juan Perez, he explained his planned voyage.

"I am tired of waiting in Spain," said Columbus. "Perhaps I will have better luck with the king of France."

"You must not do that!" Perez protested. "I believe in your plan! You must sail for Spain!"

"What can I do?" Columbus asked. "I have been in Spain for years without receiving a favorable reply from the king and queen. I do not believe I will ever receive a favorable reply — at least as long as the war is on."

"Let me see what I can do," the Franciscan responded. "I used to be the queen's confessor. I will go to court and ask Her Majesty to speak to you again."

"What will you tell the queen?"

"I will tell Her Majesty that a great opportunity will be lost if you are forced to leave Spain. Promise me that you will remain here at the monastery until I return."

"I promise," Columbus agreed.

Perez succeeded in persuading Queen Isabella to recall Columbus. The meeting ended in another failure. But this time Columbus's plan was not the stumbling-block. Some of the queen's advisers had changed their minds and now favored the voyage.

This time the queen objected to some of the demands Columbus had made. He wanted the titles of admiral and viceroy of the king. He also wanted one-tenth of the income from the lands he discovered. And he asked for his son, Diego, to have the right to inherit his titles as well as becoming a page at court.

"Master Columbus, you are asking a high price," said Isabella.

"Only what I am worth," Columbus replied proudly.

"Well, I will think it over."

Again Columbus had to wait. Then, in January of 1492, Granada fell to the Spanish armed forces. The war with the Moors was over.

This might have been a great moment for Columbus because Ferdinand and Isabella were no longer distracted by the war. Instead, Columbus was told that his proposal was finally rejected.

He left the court, determined to go to France. But one of the queen's advisers persuaded her to send a mounted messenger to overtake him and bring him back. Now Isabella informed him that she accepted his terms and that he had her support. The queen said she would pawn her jewels if necessary to pay the cost of the expedition. This proved unnecessary as Columbus had friends who were willing to put up the money. They expected to make a profit from trade with the East Indies after Columbus reached the Orient by crossing the Atlantic.

And so the great idea finally became a reality. After all the years of waiting, after all the disappointments, Columbus had what he wanted — royal backing for his voyage. He had

never given up. He had never abandoned his vision. He had shown, more than anyone else in history, the value of persistence.

Still, this was only the first step. Now it was up to him to lead the expedition across the Atlantic.

Now, without waiting, Columbus set about preparing his fleet of ships. He outfitted the ships very carefully, realizing that they would have to withstand a long ocean voyage. The selection of crews for the ships was just as important as any other choice. What kind of men would be suited to such a voyage? They would have to be fearless in the face of all the natural terrors the sea could produce — storms, hurricanes — but also be able to withstand the long, monotonous days and weeks at sea out of sight of land. These prospects scared off some of the men Columbus tried to enlist, and it was necessary to fill out the crew with prisoners. A few were murderers condemned to death. They were promised their freedom if they returned alive. With his experience of the sea, Columbus knew the type he needed to man his ships. Almost all proved to be good sailors.

It was decided that three ships should make the voyage — the *Santa Maria*, the *Pinta*, and the *Nina*. The Pinzon brothers, Martin Alonzo and Vicente Yanez, commanded the *Nina* and the *Pinta*. Columbus chose the *Santa Maria* as his flagship. The *Santa Maria* is the most famous ship in history, and yet, little is known about her except that she was the largest of the three. All of them had three masts with a large main sail slightly forward where it could catch the wind.

The pilot of the *Santa Maria*, Peralonso Nino, was one of the best at navigating the high seas. But the master of the *Santa Maria* under Columbus ran the ship aground in the Caribbean, and Columbus never trusted him after that. Luis de Torres, a Jewish convert to the Catholic Church, went along as an interpreter. Torres know Hebrew and Arabic, two languages Columbus thought would be known in the East Indies, the region of the globe where he expected to make landfall.

On August 3, 1492, at Palos, after hearing mass, Columbus ordered all aboard. The sails were unfurled and the *Santa Maria*, the *Pinta*, and the *Nina* moved out of the harbor. Soon

they were on the high seas amid surging waves with sea birds circling around.

Until the very end, some members of the royal court tried to prevent the departure of Columbus. The titles that the king had conferred on the Italian navigator had stirred up envy among the courtiers. Queen Isabella, however, refused to listen to them. Columbus sailed knowing he had the complete confidence of the queen of Spain.

The three ships headed for the Canary Islands. They made the passage in six days. By the time they got there, the *Pinta* was in trouble. The ship's rudder had worked loose, and she was becoming difficult to steer. Martin Alonzo Pinzon flew a signal of distress, and Columbus came aboard from the *Santa Maria*.

There was nothing to do but pause at the Canaries for repairs. When the *Pinta* was seaworthy again, the expedition set sail once more. Now the last known land was behind Columbus and his men. They sailed into the unknown. They faced the challenge of the Atlantic Ocean, not knowing what lay in front of them.

On and on they sailed, day-after-day. August passed. They were into September, and still the sea stretched to the horizon on every side.

On September 16, Juan de La Cosa called out to Columbus. "Admiral, there are weeds in the water!" The pilot pointed over the side.

Columbus looked, and saw a strange kind of vegetation. It was debris from the Sargasso Sea, a great mass of vegetation floating on the surface of the Atlantic. The ships went on until they entered the Sargasso Sea.

"Admiral, can we sail through these weeds?" La Cosa asked anxiously. "Will they not stop our ships and prevent us from getting out? Perhaps we will be marooned here forever!"

"Have no fear," said Columbus. "It is not thick enough to stop us. Keep the *Santa Maria* on course. We will lead the way through."

The *Santa Maria* cut a path through the Sargasso Sea. The *Pinta* and *Nina* followed.

Many of the men were alarmed by the sight of the weeds all around them. But gradually they got used to it. They knew that Columbus was right in saying they could navigate the Sargasso Sea. This gave them even more confidence in him.

"These weeds must come from an island," Peralonso Nino suggested. "Why don't we look for it?"

Columbus shook his head. "Because we are not in search of an island, even supposing we are near one. We are headed for the East Indies. Nothing must hold us up."

It was fortunate that the expedition did not stop to look for an island. No island was anywhere near them. They were in the middle of the Atlantic Ocean.

Even Columbus did not realize that the Sargasso Sea floats freely on the surface. But that did not matter. He was following his vision. He was determined not to stop before he got to the East Indies.

The expedition made good time as long as it was in the region of the North Atlantic trade winds. The sails billowed out and the ships scudded along. All the men on board felt pleased by their speed.

Then their course took them out of the trade winds. They ran into a calm area. The winds died down. The sails fell slack. The ships moved along at a fraction of their former speed.

One thing all sailors dread is a complete calm. That is when there is no wind strong enough to move a ship forward. The men Columbus commanded feared that this was about to happen.

"Do not worry," Columbus told them. "Our course will take us back into the trade winds. Besides we are not far from the East Indies. All we have to do is keep on going. Remember, there is a prize for the man who first sights land."

After that, they all strained their eyes as they peered into the distance. Each one hoped to win the prize. And of course they were eager to reach land and go ashore.

And as the wind picked up, they rejoiced at being out of the calm sea. Columbus was right again.

As the ships traveled onward, the men began to notice strange birds overhead. Some fluttered down and perched on the masts.

"A land bird!" cried one of the sailors. "We are near land!"

Others took up the cry. There was great rejoicing on all three ships.

Columbus ordered a sounding to be taken. A lead weight was dropped over the side at the end of a cable. If the lead struck bottom, that would mean they were moving into shallow water not far from land. The lead weight failed to touch bottom. No wonder! The Atlantic is more than 10,000 feet deep at that point!

Again the expedition ran out of the trade winds. The ships slowed down because the winds were blowing against them. Columbus used this difficulty to inspire his crew.

"You say the wind is blowing from the wrong direction — against us," he said. "You are right. But consider this. These contrary winds will be with us on our return voyage. They will fill our sails and carry us back to Spain!"

At his words, the men gave a loud "Hurrah for the admiral!"

That showed what a good judge of men Columbus was. The members of his crew had been wondering if a return voyage would be possible. Columbus removed that fear. "Onward to the East from the West" was the order of the day.

On September 25, Martin Alonzo Pinzon suddenly gave a shout from the *Pinta*. His words were heard on the *Santa Maria* and the *Nina*. "Land, land, sir! I claim the reward! I was the first to see it!"

Sailors climbed into the rigging to see where Pinzon was pointing. They all took up the shout, "Land! Land!"

Columbus ordered the course to be altered in that direction. It was dusk at the time, and night fell before they had gone very far.

Columbus ordered the three ships to slow down.

"Be careful," he warned his pilot. "There may be a reef ahead. We do not want to run aground."

Gingerly they proceeded onward during the night. All three pilots were prepared to order an immediate halt if the lead weight thrown over the side indicated that they were entering shallow water.

When the sun rose, the men looked around. There was no land in sight. Columbus kept in the same direction until the afternoon. Then he ordered a return to their former course, "That was not land, it was only a patch of sky, or perhaps a cloud on the horizon."

The crews felt the shock of disappointment. They went back to their tasks aboardship with less eagerness than during the night when land seemed near.

Columbus himself was not really disappointed. According to his calculations, they were not yet near the East Indies. He investigated the "land" Pinzon "discovered" because his calculations just might be wrong. He might be near the East Indies after all. The failure to find land in that direction merely indicated to him that his calculations were right after all.

There would be no departing from his original course after that. He headed toward the west. That was the idea he had formulated all those years ago. That was the vision that inspired him.

Onward to the East from the West!

The men on the ships did not share Columbus's vision. They followed him willingly when he showed them he was right. But they knew he was not infallible. Among the sailors, talk went like this:

"The admiral was wrong when he went looking for land the other day."

"True. He was as wrong as Pinzon."

"Now he says it was a patch of sky or a cloud. But he was as fooled as anybody."

"Maybe he's fooling himself about the location of the East Indies. Maybe we're not even close to them yet."

"Well, if he's fooling himself, he's fooling us too."

In one respect, the sailors were right, although they did not know it. Columbus *was* fooling them. He wrote down two logs of the voyage. In the first, which he kept to himself, he noted the real distance they had traveled. In the second, which he showed to his officers, he deliberately underestimated the distance. This was to keep them from worrying over the fact that they were so far from Spain.

The men still grumbled. They felt the monotony of the voyage. One day was like another. They kept the ships clean and seaworthy. Apart from that they had little to do but stare out at the sea and wonder how long this would go on.

It was an exciting day when one of the sailors hooked a dolphin while fishing over the side of the *Santa Maria*. The dolphin was large enough to give them all a meal.

Then it was back to sailing as usual. Discouragement set in among the men. Fears afflicted them that they had gone too far into the unknown. Perhaps they were nearing a point in the Atlantic from which it would be impossible to turn back!

"We should turn back now, before it is too late," the pilot of the *Pinta* called over to the pilot of the *Nina*.

"I'm with you on that," came the reply.

Juan de La Cosa, pilot of the *Santa Maria*, heard them. "I will bring this to the attention of the admiral," he called back.

Columbus, below deck at the time, did not realize what was happening until La Cosa informed him. The admiral summoned his crew on deck and addressed them.

"What is it you wish me to do?" he inquired. "Tell me plainly."

"We want you to turn the ships around and head back to Spain," came a surly reply.

Columbus raised his arms in the air in a gesture of defiance.

"I will never give such an order. I know you can mutiny and take over this ship. But if I stay aboard, I will testify against you when we get back to Spain. I represent Queen Isabella. The queen will have you hanged."

"Why shouldn't we throw you overboard?" somebody snarled.

"Because if I am not on the ship, you will still be hanged."

Silence fell. The men were thinking it over. Columbus quickly intervened. He always preferred to be agreeable rather than threatening.

"Think about the East Indies," he urged them. "When we get there, you will find all the gold you want. When we return to Spain — and I promise that we will return — we will all be in favor with the king and queen. Every man here will be a hero when he returns to his home. Every city and town will salute the heroes of the most daring voyage in history."

Columbus had a way of showing men where their best interests lay. This time he turned potential mutineers into enthusiastic followers.

"Hurrah for the admiral!" they cried.

And minutes later they were either back at work or looking over the bow of the ship for a sign that they had reached the East Indies.

With order restored aboard the *Santa Maria*, Columbus called to the *Pinta* and *Nina* that everyone should be of good heart as the voyage continued. Martin Alonzo Pinzon and Vicente Yanez Pinzon shouted back that there would be no further problems. The cheering of the two crews echoed across the water.

The vessels plowed through blue water under a clear blue sky. The sailors could see large fish darting about under the waves. An occasional dolphin broke the surface of the ocean and fell back with a splash. An increasing number of birds flew past. Some of them appeared to be land birds. The sight encouraged the men on the ship. It appeared that land could not be far away.

Fresh winds filled the sails. The flag of the admiral flew bravely from the tallest mast of the *Santa Maria*. The *Pinta* and the *Nina* flew the Pinzon flags.

The sailors spent their spare time on deck enjoying the good weather and the steady forward motion of the ships. They talked about the possibility of seeing land at any moment.

"I intend to win the prize by being the first to spot the shore," said one.

He was greeted with laughter.

"So do we all," another responded. "It could be any one of us."

Driftwood became numerous. It was not like the Sargasso Sea they had sailed through. It was not vegetation floating on the surface of the ocean. These were trees and bushes that had grown in the earth.

There was no doubt now. The *Santa Maria*, the *Pinta* and the *Nina* were nearing land.

The ships slowed down at night when visibility was poor. They feared that they might hit unseen rocks and sink. If that happened, the crews would never see Spain again.

The New World Is Discovered

At dawn on October 11, the signs of land were all around the three ships. Branches with green leaves still on them floated past. A length of bamboo was lifted from the water on board the *Pinta*. A sailor on the *Nina* recovered a bush with berries. The bush had been in the earth so recently that the berries had not had time to fall off.

True, all that the men could see was water everywhere they looked. But they knew that debris from land can float far out into the ocean. Columbus remembered the debris that floated with the Gulf Stream all the way to the Canary Islands. So, he knew they would strike land if they continued on their present course.

"I want every man on the alert," he ordered. "We have to make our own way in these waters because we have no maps to guide us. After all, we are near the East Indies."

But of course he and his men were thousands of miles from the East Indies. They were getting close to the West Indies.

"It is a great honor to be here, admiral," said Juan de La Cosa, the ship's master.

"Let us show ourselves worthy of the honor," Columbus responded.

"I am sure we all will," the master assured him. "Everyone is excited because our voyage across the Atlantic is about to end."

"Well, let everyone recall the reward for sighting land."

"Admiral, I am sure nobody has forgotten that."

"Whoever he is, he will deserve the reward," said Columbus.

Flowers new to the crewmen rose and fell on the waves during the day of October 11. But no land was sighted. Darkness fell, and the three ships moved onward. Again they moved cautiously for fear that they might enter shallow water filled with rocks.

Nobody could sleep, least of all Columbus. He kept straining his eyes over the bow of the *Santa Maria* in the hope of sighting land.

Suddenly he thought he saw something that looked like a light. He called a sailor named Pedro Gutierrez. Pointing to the spot, he asked Gutierrez if he saw anything.

"I do, Admiral, sir!"

"What do you see?"

"A light that comes and goes."

"Will you repeat that, Pedro?"

"A light which goes on and off, and sometimes disappears."

"What do you think?"

"I think that that light may be the first sign of life. It might be land. If it is, you have the honor of being the first one to see it."

But another sailor could see nothing. Columbus was mistaken. He could not have seen a light because they were too far from the nearest island in the Caribbean.

The three ships kept sailing close together so as not to lose contact with each other. On board, men kept constant watch. As Juan de La Cosa had said to Columbus, nobody wanted to miss the chance to win the prize that Columbus was authorized by Queen Isabella to offer to the first man to see land.

A little after two, in the darkness of the morning on October 12, 1492, in a silent sea, the sound of a voice echoed across the water.

The lookout aboard the *Pinta*, Rodrigo de Triana, shouted: "Land! Land! Land!"

"Where?" Martin Alonzo Pinzon demanded.

"Up ahead, sir! I see a light!"

Triana was right. Everybody on the *Pinta* saw the light, which was gleaming on a shore they were approaching.

"Land! Land! Land!" was repeated over and over again.

"The sea has been conquered!"

"We've made it! Long live Columbus!"

Pinzon ordered one of the ship's cannon to be fired. The sound told the *Santa Maria* and the *Nina* that land had really been sighted.

Columbus ordered his pilot to maneuver the *Santa Maria* close to the *Pinta*.

"Pinzon, are you sure you have sighted land?" Columbus called out.

"Absolutely, admiral. Look over there. You will see a light too."

"There's no doubt about it," Columbus agreed. "Pinzon, we are in the East Indies!"

The *Pinta* came alongside her two sister ships. All on board heard the news. The three crews were now cheering and yelling. The men slapped one another on the back.

Columbus had to call them to order. "Stay alert! We have to watch out for ships as well as rocks! Don't run into an East Indian ship when we're just at the end of our voyage!"

This was one danger that they did not need to worry about. The American Indians did not build ships that large. Their canoes would have been no threat to the large vessels from Europe.

All the misconceptions Columbus believed came from his vision of a landfall in the East Indies. Of course the men under his command did not doubt his word — not when he had brought them safely this far.

October 12, 1492. This is one of the memorable dates in human history — the date of the discovery of the New World. Today it is commemorated by the nations of North and South America as Columbus Day.

As dawn broke, the shores of an island came into view. Columbus and his men saw a beach where the surf of the Atlantic Ocean rolled up over the sand, came to a halt, and rolled back. Beyond the beach stood tall trees surrounded by the lush green vegetation of the Caribbean.

"Admiral, there must be people living here," the pilot of the *Santa Maria* commented.

"Undoubtedly, La Cosa," Columbus said. "Otherwise there wouldn't be a fire for us to see. They must be back in the woods."

"I wonder if they are friendly."

"We will soon find out. There isn't any reason why they shouldn't be friendly. Marco Polo traveled all over the Far East, and he says nothing of hostile peoples in the East Indies."

"I wonder if Marco Polo reached this island."

"Probably not. It would be a strange coincidence if he visited the one island where we

happened to make our landfall. We will see for ourselves if the islanders will make us welcome."

"What do we do now, admiral?"

"We take care of our ships. Signal Martin Alonzo Pinzon. Tell him to sail along the coast of the island and look for a place to drop anchor. We must have shallow water without rocks."

Pinzon did as he was ordered. As he sailed the *Pinta* along the shore, he edged away from any area that was rocky. He took constant soundings with a weighted lead to make sure the water was deep enough to float his ship but not too deep for the anchor to reach the bottom and keep it from floating away.

The *Pinta* came to a cove, a place where the shore curved inward. Projecting spits of land at either end of the curve enclosed an expanse of placid water. The depth was enough to float a ship but not too deep for an anchor to reach the bottom and keep it from floating away.

Pinzon fired his cannon as a signal to the rest of the expedition. The *Santa Maria* and the *Nina* quickly joined the *Pinta*.

The three ships anchored together in the cove. Columbus held a consultation with the two Pinzon brothers. They agreed with him that this was the place to stay until they could land and find out what kind of an island they had reached.

All of the sailors were eager to go ashore. Most of them, however, were compelled to stay and look after the ships while a small party went in landing craft to the beach.

Three small boats were lowered into the water, one for Columbus and one for each of the Pinzons. Each of them took a few men with him. To the admiral went the honor of being the first European to set foot in the New World. He knelt in the sand as his captains came ashore behind him.

"I take possession of this land," he said in a strong voice, "in the name of Queen Isabella and King Ferdinand of Spain."

Then with a firm movement, he made a small hole with the tip of his sword and planted the flag of the *Santa Maria*.

He summoned a notary to his side to record his words: "I will name this island San Salvador; you have heard me state this in front of two witnesses — Martin Alonzo and Vicente Pinzon. Notary take note!"

Then, still kneeling with all those around him, he asked them to accept these solemn words: "I vow to obey the viceroy of these newly discovered lands, the admiral of the Great Ocean, the governor of the Indies."

"We do," they shouted.

At that moment, there was a rustling of leaves and several mysterious beings emerged from the forest. They walked forward cautiously, but their curiosity was stronger than their fear. They had come to observe the movements of the equally mysterious beings who had disembarked from the huge, strange ships.

As soon as they saw the Spaniards and realized that they were human beings too, they rushed up to express their respect and their joy.

Columbus turned to his interpreter, who knew Hebrew and Arabic, and asked him to speak to the natives of the island. The natives, however, could not speak either language. This disappointed Columbus because he thought at least one of the two languages would be known in the East Indies. If only he had known that he was nowhere near the East Indies!

But the Spaniards, though they could not communicate with the natives, were fascinated by them — by their nudity, their ruddy skins, their short, straight hair, their docile behavior. They did not carry any arms and they did not seem to know anything about the Spanish, assuming they had come from the sea itself.

Columbus ordered that the "Indians" (he called them that because he thought he was in the East Indies) be given the various trinkets he had brought with him from Spain.

Then joiners and carpenters from the ship worked together to build a great crucifix which Columbus planted on a rise where all could see it.

"I bring my own name to the destiny of this cross," he said, alluding to the fact that he was named after St. Christopher, the bearer of Christ.

The island that Columbus named San Salvador was known to the Indians as Guanahani. Today it is Watling Island on the map of the Bahamas.

This tiny speck of land off the coast of Florida has little importance in itself. It has no strategic position in the Bahamas, and no gift of natural resources. What it does have is a series of beautiful beaches — and a unique place in history as the island where Columbus came ashore when he discovered America.

The New World

Columbus spent two days at San Salvador. The Indians became bolder as they began to mingle with the strange visitors with the pale skins who had come to their island so suddenly.

The Indians were Arawaks, members of a large group that migrated from South America and overran Cuba and Haiti as well as the Bahamas. They were not savages. They knew how to spin cloth, mold pottery, and build sturdy huts in which to live.

They armed themselves with short spears, which they needed to defend themselves against the brutal Caribs (who gave their name to the Caribbean). The Arawaks of San Salvador were not warlike. If left to themselves, they would have lived in peace.

One thing in particular caught the attention of the Spaniards. These natives wore gold ornaments with which they were willing to part. The natives were in fact quite friendly, and proceeded to happily trade with the Spaniards, offering them rings and pendants of real gold in exchange for trinkets of no value. The expedition had brought three cargoes of trinkets for just this type of trade.

"We should try to convert these people to our faith," said a friar who had made the journey.

"Of course, father," Columbus said. "That was one reason for this voyage, as you know — to convert the heathen to the Catholic faith. I will give you all the assistance I can once we have established ourselves here."

"But how are we going to keep the crews from collecting booty?" asked one sailor. "They are already so impatient."

"And so greedy," commented Columbus.

"But we've come to this land. We can control these people. Don't we have a right to take whatever we want for ourselves?" asked a sailor.

"We are here to enrich ourselves, too," Columbus admitted. "But we must not be hasty. There is no point in making enemies if we do not have to. Let us be friendly to them until we discover where their gold comes from. That is something I mean to try and find out if I can."

"But they don't mind trading their gold to us. Why shouldn't we buy as much as we can from them right now."

"I do not oppose trading," said Columbus. "I just don't want to antagonize them."

"But we promised to bring riches to the king," said the notary.

"I have not forgotten my duty," Columbus retorted. "I simply intend to maintain order while we are here on this island."

He was indeed worried about their greed for the natives' gold. There was so much gold in their earrings, necklaces, bracelets and other ornaments. But it was because of this precious metal that some of his crew committed themselves to journey farther on, into the heart of Eldorado — the land of gold.

This was why it was so easy for Columbus to persuade his men to follow him. After all, this was only one island. There must be others. And if there was gold on one, why not on all of them?

Columbus was not simply a man with a mystical vision. He was also a practical man who intended to gain riches for Spain, for his followers — and for himself.

The "Indies"

Three days after landing at San Salvador, Columbus began to explore the nearby islands. Wherever he went he used sign language to communicate with the men and women he met. All were "Indians" to him, just as all the islands belonged to the "Indies," meaning the East Indies.

To one island he gave the name Isabella in honor of the queen of Spain. Here he saw a chief wearing a robe studded with gold. The climate was so pleasant and the vegetation so lush — flowers and trees blooming in profusion — that he was moved to exclaim: "I could never tire of looking at all these amazing things!"

He saw birds and animals that he had never seen before. The natives introduced him to strange plants, some of which had valuable medicinal properties. He stayed an extra two days on enchanting Isabella Island, partly because he liked it and partly because the Indian chief invited him to stay and explore.

Eventually Columbus came to the biggest island of the Caribbean, Cuba. Its size made him think that it might be part of the mainland — an exciting prospect because, of course, he thought the mainland would be China or possibly Japan.

Columbus even sent out a search party to see if they could find the capital city of the Great Khan — the emperor. The search party returned empty-handed. This was another disappointment to Columbus who wanted to pay his respects to the Great Khan in the name of the king of Spain.

While he was on Cuba, a disturbing incident occurred. The *Pinta* vanished. Martin Alonzo Pinzon felt critical of the way Columbus was exploring the island. The Spanish captain had been informed by an Indian guide that an island filled with gold was nearby. He did not find the golden island — the guide's tale was false.

Columbus guessed Pinzon's motive. The two did not meet again for nearly two months.

Surprised by the size of Cuba, an island without a ruler, Columbus ordered his notary to write down all the relevant facts. On one occasion he dictated for the information of the king of Spain: "No white man and no Christian has ever come here before, and the land is ripe for conversion to our glorious Christian religion."

For all his interest in new lands and in gold, Columbus never forgot his commitment to the religious purpose of his voyage. He had missionaries with him, and they made the first converts in the New World.

This became easier as the Spaniards learned a little of the island languages. Communication was no longer so much of a problem, although some sign language remained necessary.

Wherever he stopped, Columbus would gather the Indians together in their villages or on the beaches. Then his missionaries would preach to the assembled crowd. More and more Indians professed their faith in the Catholic religion.

Columbus was overjoyed that he was an instrument of God in bringing the true faith to the heathen.

From Cuba, Columbus sailed to another large island. He called it Hispaniola. We know it today as the Caribbean island shared by the countries of Haiti and the Dominican Republic.

Remaining on board the *Santa Maria*, Columbus sent an exploration party ashore.

"Go as far inland as you can in a day or two," he instructed the leader of the party. "See what the people are like. If they have gold, try to find out from them where it comes from. If there are gold mines on Hispaniola, make a chart so we can find them again."

"Admiral, we'll do our best and report back to you," the leader vowed.

The search party discovered a number of villages. They met Indians who wore costumes decorated with gold. But they returned to the *Santa Maria* without finding any gold mines. They did find nuggets in the streams, but not in the amounts the Spaniards were looking for.

The Spaniards did not know that the large gold ornaments worn by the people of the Caribbean came from Mexico and Central America. The mainland Indians traded gold ornaments to the people of the nearest islands. These people then traded the gold ornaments to the Indian islands farther out in the Caribbean. The Spaniards did not find enormous amounts of gold until they conquered Mexico.

The search party Columbus sent out reported to him that Hispaniola lacked gold but was otherwise a place worth holding.

"It has an abundance of food and water, admiral," the leader said. "The streams are filled with fish. Banana trees grow everywhere."

"And the people?" Columbus asked.

"Very peaceful. They will not make any trouble for us."

Columbus kept this point in mind when a crowd of Indians came down onto the shore. An Indian leader and some of his followers came aboard the *Santa Maria*. Columbus gave them a meal and talked to them.

Afterward, he said to Juan de La Cosa: "We can control these people. They will make ideal slaves because they will not resist us."

This showed a great failing of Columbus. He believed in slavery. He saw nothing wrong with enslaving the American Indians and making them work for Spanish masters.

This unfortunately became a policy of the Spaniards who followed Columbus to the New World. They converted the Indians to the Catholic faith. But they also kept them as slaves. Missionaries protested against this policy, but they were not listened to.

Hispaniola provided food and water. The people were peaceful. Partly for these reasons Columbus made a decision. He summoned his men to inform them what he intended to do.

"I am going to found a settlement here. Some of you will stay while I return to Spain. But you will not be forgotten. I will bring men to replace you when I come back here on my next voyage."

"Admiral, are you sure there will be another voyage?" a sailor asked doubtfully.

"I am sure. The king and queen of Spain have made me their viceroy in these islands. I will return to establish my authority here. In fact, I am planning several voyages. There are more islands to explore. And I intend to reach the mainland some day."

Under his directions, his men built thatched huts like those the Indians of Hispaniola lived in. Some of the Indians were put to work on the huts, showing their skill at this type of construction.

Although the people were peaceful, Columbus ordered a defensive wall to be built all around the huts. He was worried in case hostile Indians should arrive and attack his settlement. The defensive wall was made up mostly of tall, heavy tree trunks.

The result was a stockade — a group of huts where men could live and where they could defend themselves if they were attacked. Columbus assigned thirty-nine men to remain in the settlement. They would have to take care of themselves in this strange place. They would see no other white men until his return.

Columbus called the settlement La Navidad. It was the first European settlement in the New World.

He hoped it would be a permanent colony on the island. So, on his second voyage to the New World, he made for Hispaniola to visit the men he had left.

When he returned it was a sad day for him. He found that La Navidad was gone. The men had disappeared. The stockade was burned to the ground.

Columbus made an inquiry among the Indians. He found out that some of the men he had left became bandits. They left the stockade in search of women and gold. They ignored the complaints of the Indians.

The Spaniards attacked a group of Indians who were not peaceful. These Indians then attacked the stockade. They killed the Spaniards and wiped out the European settlement.

So ended La Navidad. Its fate was a tragedy for Columbus.

Before establishing the settlement at La Navidad, Columbus had suffered a terrible blow while sailing along the coast of Hispaniola.

On Christmas eve, 1492, the Santa Maria ran aground.

Columbus was asleep in his cabin at the time. Master Juan de La Cosa was in charge of the ship. But La Cosa decided to sleep, too, instead of remaining on watch. He left another man to steer the Santa Maria.

They were sailing along a part of the coast where a coral reef extended underwater from

the shore out into the deep water. Suddenly the *Santa Maria* drove up on top of the reef and skidded to a stop.

The alarm bell sounded. Everyone on board was jarred awake. Columbus came rushing up on deck.

"What's wrong?" he shouted.

"We're grounded on a reef, admiral!" said Juan de La Cosa.

"How did it happen?"

"I don't know. I was asleep."

"You were what?" Columbus demanded furiously.

La Cosa was embarrassed. "It was my fault, admiral."

"It certainly was," Columbus accused him. "Well, let's see if we can get her off the reef."

All efforts to float the *Santa Maria* into deep water failed. The ship was wedged too tightly onto the coral reef.

Huge waves rolled against the *Santa Maria*. They drove her further onto the reef. She rose with the waves and then fell back on the sharp coral with a thump.

The timbers of the *Santa Maria* gave way. Water poured in. Soon it became clear that she was a total loss.

Columbus and the crew of the *Santa Maria* transferred to the *Nina*. He decided to found La Navidad partly because of the loss of the *Santa Maria*. The *Nina* was not large enough for two crews, and so he assigned the men of his ruined flagship to the settlement in Hispaniola. Timbers salvaged from the *Santa Maria* were used in building La Navidad's stockade.

So ended the flagship of Columbus, the most famous ship in history — the *Santa Maria*.

While work on La Navidad was going on, the *Pinta* suddenly appeared off the coast of Hispaniola. An Indian reported this to Columbus, who sent a message to Martin Alonzo Pinzon inviting him to rejoin the expedition. Pinzon, having failed to find the gold he craved, did so.

On January 16, 1493, the *Pinta* and the *Nina* set sail out into the Atlantic. Now aboard the *Nina*, Columbus used this vessel as his flagship for the return voyage. He brought a group of Indians with him to show to King Ferdinand and Queen Isabella.

There was no grumbling on either ship this time.

"The Admiral got us safely across the ocean, and he will get us safely back to Spain." Such was the feeling among both crews.

This time they were not sailing into the unknown. There was no need to fear what lay ahead. They were simply recrossing an ocean familiar to them.

"The men are singing at their work, admiral," said Vicente Yanez Pinzon to Columbus.

"They have good reason to sing," Columbus replied. "They are on their way home. They're anxious to get there. And to tell you the truth, so am I."

"And I, too, admiral."

Experts in navigation say that the seamanship of Columbus was more remarkable on the return voyage than on the voyage to America.

That was because of the storms he ran into. At one time, he had to maneuver the sails of the *Nina* back and forth to make headway against gale-force winds blowing in his face. At another time, side winds blew the *Nina* off-course, and Columbus had to let her scud before them.

But he stuck to his route so well that he scarcely lost any time in his long run across the Atlantic.

The Viceroy

One storm arose when the Nina and the Pinta were approaching the Azores. The two ships had managed to stay together until then. Now the high winds, huge waves and torrential rain separated them. They lost sight of one another.

Columbus ordered a landing in the Azores to wait for better weather.

"Admiral, there's no sign of the Pinta," Vicente Yanez Pinzon observed.

"Your brother is a good sailor," Columbus responded. "He will bring his ship into Palos."

The Nina left the Azores. Columbus was intending to sail straight to Spain, but a second heavy storm battered the Nina off Portugal. Columbus had to run into the mouth of the Tagus River to make repairs.

Columbus sent word of his arrival to the king of Portugal. King John II invited him to come to court. There Columbus described his achievement.

"Your Majesty, I have reached the East Indies by sailing west across the Atlantic."

"I should have supported your voyage," the king confessed. "Then your discoveries would have belonged to Portugal instead of Spain. Well, you are a brave man, Columbus. You may continue your journey back to Spain. Ferdinand and Isabella will be pleased to hear what you have done."

"You are most generous, Your Majesty," said Columbus.

Leaving the Portuguese court, he hurried back to the Nina. He feared that King John II might change his mind and make him a prisoner. The king of Portugal might even keep the success of Columbus a secret. He might send a fleet across the Atlantic to exploit the lands Columbus had discovered.

As soon as the Nina was seaworthy, Columbus ordered anchor to be lifted. The ship sailed out of the Tagus River into the Atlantic.

His route now took him south along the Portuguese coast. He made the turn east into Spanish waters in the Gulf of Cadiz. On March 15, 1493, his ship entered the harbor of Palos. The crew burst into cheers.

Vicente Yanez Pinzon spoke emotionally. "Admiral, what things have we not seen and done since we left this harbor. It is a tribute to you."

"And to you Vicente Yanez. And to your brother Martin Alonzo. And to all the men who sailed with us."

Columbus was generous in giving praise to others. But at the same time, he always wanted the honors that were due to himself.

As he sailed into Palos harbor, he was afraid that Martin Alonzo Pinzon might have already arrived in the Pinta. What if Martin Alonzo was already on his way to the Spanish court? What if he was already there and claiming to be the real hero of the transatlantic voyage?

Columbus scanned the harbor for the Pinta. She was not there. Columbus breathed more freely. The Nina had beaten the Pinta home.

But not by much. The Nina was scarcely at anchor at Palos before the Pinta came sailing in.

Since Columbus had sent messages overland from Portugal to Spain, the people of Palos were ready for a celebration. The sailors were entertained at banquets. They told their stories over and over again.

Columbus had left Palos prepared for a voyage lasting a year. His round trip had taken only thirty-two weeks. That was very little time in those days for a major expedition. Quick return of this expedition showed that it had been directed by a genius.

Already people were calling Columbus the "Great Navigator."

From Palos, Columbus went to the royal court in Barcelona. We noted at the start of this book how he, his men, and his Indians were greeted by enthusiastic crowds. We saw how King Ferdinand and Queen Isabella received him and loaded him with honors.

They gave him the rank of a nobleman. They said in a royal proclamation that he had a right to the titles "admiral of the Great Ocean" and "governor of the islands and the mainland."

These titles meant that Columbus would have complete control in the lands he had discovered. In Spain he was under the authority of the king, the queen, and their appointed advisers. Once on the high seas, he would be his own master.

This was important because Ferdinand and Isabella quickly approved a second voyage. Before he was through, Columbus sailed to the New World four times.

Everyone knows the story of Columbus and the egg. The incident is said to have occurred while he was at the royal court in Barcelona after his first voyage.

He was at dinner with some Spanish noblemen, according to the story. One of the guests denied the importance of the voyage. His argument was that if Columbus had not crossed the Atlantic, another sea captain would have.

In reply, Columbus challenged all of them to make a hard-boiled egg stand upright. The egg passed from hand-to-hand around the table. They all tried to balance the egg on one end. Naturally, they all failed.

The egg circled around the table and came back to Columbus. He then cracked the large end, and placed that end on the table. Of course the egg stood upright.

"Gentlemen, now that I have shown you how to do it," said Columbus, "any of you can do it. And now that I have crossed the Atlantic, any sea captain can cross the Atlantic. The important person in any endeavor is the one who succeeds first."

The discoveries of Columbus created one embarrassment for Ferdinand and Isabella. Portugal had claims on islands in the Atlantic south of the Canaries and west of Africa.

"Your Majesty," said an adviser to King Ferdinand, "the Portuguese may contest our rights to the lands discovered by Columbus. King John II could be planning to send an expedition across the Atlantic right now."

"What do you propose that I do?"

"Ask the pope to decide. Let him draw a line on the map dividing the territories overseas. If the Portuguese agree, their exploring expeditions will not threaten our territories. Nor will our exploring expeditions threaten theirs."

"A good idea," said Ferdinand. "Propose this plan in Rome and in Lisbon."

Negotiations with Pope Alexander VI and King John II of Portugal were successful. Out of the negotiations came the Demarcation Line, which the pope drew on the map of the Atlantic Ocean.

Everything east of the Demarcation Line belonged to Portugal. Everthing west of it belonged to Spain. The Demarcation Line cut through the "hump" of South America. That gave to Portugal the land that later became Brazil. The rest of the Americas went to Spain.

By a later treaty between Spain and Portugal, the line was shifted to the west. But Portugal did not gain any more territory by this agreement. The Portuguese colonized Brazil, where Portuguese is still spoken. The Spaniards colonized the rest of Latin America, and the people there still speak Spanish.

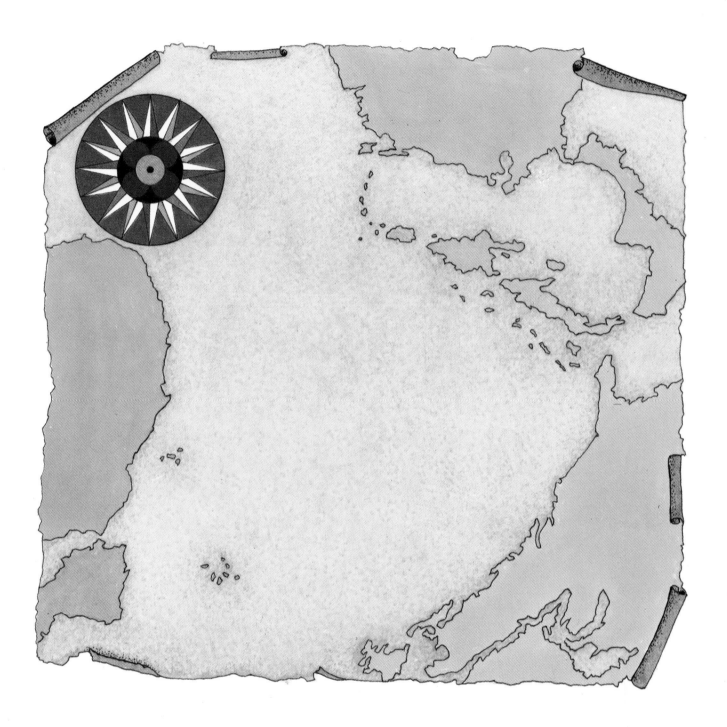

Thus, Columbus was able to undertake his second voyage across the Atlantic without fearing that a Portuguese expedition would oppose him. The two nations of the Iberian Peninsula kept their words. Neither tried to take advantage of the other while they were exploring overseas.

Columbus immediately prepared for his second voyage. Ferdinand and Isabella gave him a large expedition — 17 ships and more than 1,200 men.

Quite a difference from the *Santa Maria*, the *Pinta*, and the *Nina* of the first voyage!

On his second voyage, beginning on October 13, 1493, Columbus found that his settlement of La Navidad on Hispaniola had been destroyed. To replace it, he established Isabela, which became the first European city in the Americas.

He discovered Puerto Rico and Jamaica while exploring the Caribbean. But he had trouble with his followers, who considered him dictatorial. The Indians became rebellious because he compelled them to hand over their gold. He thus was in difficulties when he got back to Spain on June 11, 1495.

The third voyage of Columbus began on May 30, 1498. This time he headed south and discovered Trinidad and the coast of South America. Then he returned to Hispaniola.

However, complaints against Columbus in Spain caused Ferdinand and Isabella to send a governor, Francisco de Bobadilla, to replace him. Bobadilla had Columbus arrested and sent back to Spain in chains. The king and queen ordered his release. After hearing his story, they rewarded him for his contribution to the greatness of Spain.

They also allowed him to make a fourth voyage, which started on May 9, 1502. This time he coasted along Central America. He passed by the land that is now occupied by Honduras, Nicaragua, Costa Rica, and Panama. Later explorers added to his achievement. They discovered more unknown places by following where he had led the way.

The map on the opposite page reveals how one geographer put the facts together as far as he could understand them. This geographer believed Columbus was right in saying that Cuba was attached to the mainland. Later explorations proved Cuba was an island.

Columbus returned to Spain for the last time in May, 1505. Although very ill from the hardships he had suffered, he still hoped to sail on a fifth voyage. When he arrived at court, his great protector, Queen Isabella, was dead. King Ferdinand refused to approve another transatlantic expedition.

Columbus suffered through this final disappointment. He died in Valladolid on May 20, 1506.

To the day of his death, he insisted that he had reached the East by sailing West. He believed the islands he had discovered were part of the East Indies. He cherished the thought that a fifth voyage, had it been possible, might have allowed him to land in China.

We know that the feat of the Great Navigator was much more important than that — Columbus discovered America.

The Admiral of the Great Ocean

In search of support for his "great enterprise," Christopher Columbus wrote to King Ferdinand of Spain. This letter, marked by faith and confidence, shows the courage of Columbus in offering to prove that he could reach Asia by sailing from the Occident ("onward to the East from the West"). This is part of what he said:

I have been a navigator since childhood. I have roamed the seas for many years. I have explored every part of the known world and have spoken with many: with religious, with seculars, with people of every faith, with Latins, Greeks, and Moors. I have acquired a knowledge of navigation, astronomy, and geometry; I am an expert cartographer who can draw up a map of the world. I can show the location of cities, rivers, mountains, and all manner of places as they really are. I have studied cosmography, history, and philosophy. I am certain I can reach the Indies, and I respectfully request Your Majesty to approve my enterprise. If Your Highness will grant me the means to execute my plans, no obstacle will stop me from making a success of this enterprise.

In April 1492, Ferdinand was convinced of the merit of Columbus' plan and approved it. In less than three months, Columbus managed to equip three ships: the *Nina*, the *Pinta*, and the *Santa Maria*. Columbus sailed from Palos on August 3, 1492, on his immortal enterprise with the title "admiral of the Great Ocean."

Model of the flagship of the expedition of Christopher Columbus: the *Santa Maria*. The model is in the Historical Naval Museum of Venice. The original is in Vienna.

The Discovery of the "Indies"

Christopher Columbus did not know that he had discovered a new world. He firmly believed that he had found the shortest route to the land of gold, to those Indies that Marco Polo had described in his marvelous diaries. In fact, this is why Columbus called the natives "Indians," the peaceful people of the islands he discovered. He loved the natural beauty of these lands. He claimed them in the name of the Cross and of the king of Spain. Here is part of a letter to the Spanish monarch in which he describes Haiti (which he called Hispaniola):

All the islands are fertile, but this one is the measure by which they may be judged. The coastline has harbors superior to many I have seen in Europe, and there are great rivers on the island. The land is high and there are some spectacular mountain chains, taller than those of Tenerife. And everything is beautiful, lush, and fertile. There are hundreds of varieties of trees, some so high they seem to touch the sky. There are seven or eight varieties of palms alone, stunning in their beauty, and many evergreens. There are thousands of herbs and plants. I have seen an extraordinary number of pines and broad fields of cultivated crops. There are honey and many types of birds and fruit. In the interior of the island, there must be mines to account for the metals that the inhabitants of the place use.

After his discovery of America, Columbus made three more voyages of exploration. They are outlined on the map below. In September of 1493, he returned to discover Puerto Rico and Jamaica. In 1498, his third voyage brought him to Trinidad and the coast of South America near the mouth of the Orinoco River. On his fourth voyage, in 1502, he discovered Central America and explored along the isthmus.

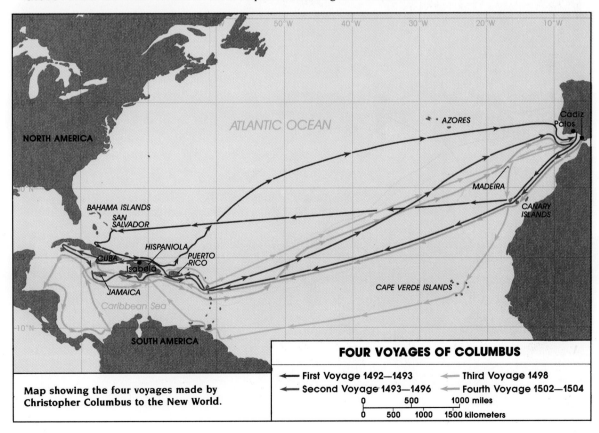

Map showing the four voyages made by Christopher Columbus to the New World.

FOUR VOYAGES OF COLUMBUS

← First Voyage 1492—1493	← Third Voyage 1498
← Second Voyage 1493—1496	← Fourth Voyage 1502—1504

0   500   1000 miles

0   500   1000   1500 kilometers

Antecdotes about Christopher Columbus

I — The Coat of Arms of the Viceroy. As a boy, Columbus lived for awhile in the city of Siena, near the Church of Fontegiusta. It was at this time that he saw a girl in this church with whom he fell in love. Her wealthy family opposed the relationship since Columbus came from a modest family. The last time he saw his first love, believing he would have a glorious future, she said to him: "Send me news of your adventures." The news was long in coming, but after many years there arrived at the church a votive gift from the admiral of the Great Ocean: the coat of arms of Columbus as viceroy of Spain in the New World he had discovered.

That coat of arms was placed in the Church of Fontegiusta. The girl he had once met in that church recognized the name of Christopher Columbus.

II — The Eclipse in Jamaica. In need of food and fresh water, Columbus was once forced to drop anchor at Jamaica. But the natives there were extremely hostile.

Realizing that there was to be a lunar eclipse that night, Columbus spoke to them in these terms: "I am not hostile to you. All I want is food and water for my men. Let me have them. If you refuse, I will put out the moon and that will be the beginning of many misfortunes for you and your island." The natives opposed the admiral of the Great Ocean. But when they saw the moon vanish in the night sky, they fell on their knees. Trembling, they let Columbus have what he needed to continue his voyage.

Antique print illustrating the story, concerning Christopher Columbus, famous as "the egg of Columbus." This story, for which there is no real proof, is described in this book.

"We Give You Forever"

The king of Spain had to obtain the pope's permission to accept jurisdiction over the lands Columbus discovered. Here is part of the papal bull, addressed to King Ferdinand, giving Columbus the right to take these lands for Spain:

We know well that you intended to search for and to find islands and remote lands, both known and unknown, and to bring the inhabitants to the Catholic faith, and that you have not had time to complete so holy and benevolent a work. We know, finally, that to achieve this you invited our well-loved son, Christopher Columbus — a man certainly worthy of responsibility for such an enterprise — to go with ships and men, not without great fatigue and danger, to discover lands and remote islands and to sail into seas never navigated before...

I see in particular the scope of this achievement, and of the spreading of the Christian faith...and I recognize that under the guidance of divine providence lands and islands are being found, and their inhabitants led into the Catholic faith.

And considering the importance of this work, freely and without any other motive, through our own initiative, by our generosity, and our apostolic authority, we give to you forever and to your successors (King of Castile and of Leon), through the authority of God omnipotent and our gift, all the islands and the lands, discovered and to be discovered, known and unknown, in the Occident, limited by a line traced from the Arctic Pole to the Antarctic Pole.

We command you to send to these lands and islands just men, moved by fear of God, expert in instructing the inhabitants in the Catholic faith and educating them in moral behavior.

In his turn, the king, to the eternal glory of Columbus, gave the Great Navigator a heraldic coat of arms in which the castle of Castile and the lion of Leon occupied the two upper quarters. The two lower quarters showed islands in the midst of an ocean and five anchors representing the voyages of the admiral of the Great Ocean. The opposite side of the coat of arms bore the words in Spanish:

Por Castilla y por Leon — Nuevo Mondo hallo Colon

Translated, this means: Columbus discovered a new world for the glory of the sovereigns of Castile (the castle of Isabella) and Aragon (the lion of Ferdinand).

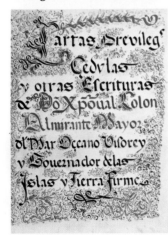

Text of the privileges bestowed on Christopher Columbus by King Ferdinand and Queen Isabella.

HISTORICAL CHRONOLOGY

Life of Columbus	Historical and Cultural Events
	1446 Death of Filippo Brunelleschi, leading Renaissance artist.
	1450 Johann Gutenberg perfects printing with movable type.
1451 Born in Genoa, exact date unknown.	
	1452 Birth of Leonardo da Vinci.
	1453 End of Hundred Years War between England and France, notable for leadership of Joan of Arc. Constantinople falls to the Turks.
	1455 Outbreak of Wars of the Roses, civil wars in England.
	1469 Isabella of Castile marries Ferdinand of Aragon, unifying Spain. Birth of Niccolo Machiavelli, political philosopher.
1472 Sails to North Africa.	
1473 Sails to Greek island of Chios.	**1473** Birth of Copernicus, father of modern astronomy.
	1475 Printing of Ptolemy's *Guide to Geography*, which stimulates European exploration.

House where Columbus spent his childhood in Genoa. Restored in 1700.

Joan of Arc on horseback — Medieval French miniature.

Silver crown of Isabella the Catholic — Fifteenth century.

Benin culture — Bronze figures in high relief forming a procession.

Life of Columbus	Historical and Cultural Events
1476 In battle off Cape Saint Vincent, swims six miles to Portuguese coast with aid of floating oar.	
1477 Sails to Iceland.	
1478 Marries Filipa Perestrello.	
	1483 Birth of Raphael, one of the world's greatest artists.
1484 King John II of Portugal rejects his plan to reach the East Indies by sailing west across the Atlantic.	
1485 Columbus goes to Spain.	**1485** End of Wars of the Roses with victory of Henry VII.
1486 Meets King Ferdinand and Queen Isabella.	**1486** Affonso d'Aveira, Portuguese explorer, travels up Niger River in West Africa.
1488 King John II rejects his plan again.	**1488** Bartholomew Dias, Portuguese sea captain, rounds Cape of Good Hope, opening a sea route to India.
1489 Columbus returns to Spain.	
1492 Ferdinand and Isabella approve his plan; he sails to America, lands on Guanahani (San Salvador), discovers Cuba and Hispaniola, loses the *Santa Maria*.	**1492** Death of Lorenzo the Magnificent, dictator of Florence.

Raphael — *Madonna of the Chair.* Done on wood.

Cape of Good Hope, discovered by Bartholomew Dias.

Lorenzo the Magnificent — **Portrait by Georgio Vasari.**

Leonardo da Vinci — *The Last Supper.* Figure of Jesus. Fresco in tempera.

Life of Columbus	Historical and Cultural Events
1493 Returns to Spain aboard the *Nina* followed by the *Pinta*; receives a hero's welcome; departs on his second voyage during which he discovers Puerto Rico and Jamaica.	**1493** Papal bull places Demarcation Line on map of the world, dividing discovered and undiscovered between Spain and Portugal. Birth of Paracelsus, pioneer of modern chemistry.
1494 Faces discontent among his men on Hispaniola but manages to control it.	**1494** Spain and Portugal agree to shift Demarcation Line farther west. Spain and France begin war for domination of Italy.
1495 Returns to Spain.	**1495** Leonardo da Vinci begins work on *The Last Supper*.
	1496 Joanna the Mad, daughter of Ferdinand and Isabella, marries Philip the Handsome of Austria, uniting Habsburg lands with those of Spain.
	1497 John Cabot, Venetian sea captain sailing for England, reaches the coast of North America.
1498 Departs on his third voyage during which he discovers Trinidad and South America.	**1498** Vasco da Gama, Portuguese sea captain, sails around the Cape of Good Hope to India.
1499 New governor sends Columbus back to Spain in chains; he is liberated and rewarded by Ferdinand and Isabella.	**1499** Michelangelo finishes his *Pieta* in Rome.

Treaty of Tordesillas between Spain and Portugal — signed page.

Francis I on the throne — French miniature of the period.

Joanna the Mad — Portrait by Michel Sittow — Sixteenth century.

Michelangelo — Sculpture of the *Pieta*.

Life of Columbus	Historical and Cultural Events
	1500 Pedro Cabral, Portuguese sea captain, discovers Brazil.
1502 Departs on his fourth voyage during which he discovers Central America.	
1504 Returns to Spain ill and exhausted.	
	1505 Death of Ivan the Great, founder of modern Russia.
1506 Columbus dies in Valladolid.	
	1507 Martin Waldseemuller, German geographer, names New World after Venetian explorer, Amerigo Vespucci: AMERICA.
	1517 Portuguese reach Canton by sea and sign commercial agreement between Portugal and China.
	1533 Francisco Pizarro, Spanish conqueror, executes Atahualpa, Inca king, and imposes Spanish rule on Peru.
	1536 Henry VIII executes Ann Boleyn, the woman for whom he broke with the Catholic Church.
	1547 Birth of Miguel de Cervantes, author of *Don Quixote*.

Andrea Palladio — Entrance to the Olympic Theater in Venice.

Pizarro and his men battle the Indians. Print by T. de Bray.

Henry VIII jousts in the presence of his wife, Catherine of Aragon — Miniature.

Miguel de Cervantes — *Don Quixote*. Illustrated by G. Dore

SOURCES

Original documents:

Major, J.R. (ed.), *Four Voyages to the New World* (1847,
reprint 1961) — writings of Columbus

Secondary authorities:

Bradford, Ernle, *Christopher Columbus* (1947)
Hale, J.R., *Renaissance Exploration* (1968)
Morison, Samuel Eliot, *Admiral of the Ocean Sea: A Life
of Christopher Columbus* (1942)
Skelton, R.A., *Explorers' Maps* (1958)

1 2 3 4 5 6 7 8 9 10—IL—93 92 91 90 89 88 87 86 85